'nsync now & forever

backstage pass

By A. Pearl

SCHOLASTIC INC.

New York   Toronto   London   Auckland   Sydney
Mexico City   New Delhi   Hong Kong

Front cover: Clavel/A.P.R.F./Shooting Star; back cover: London Features; page 1: London Features; page 3: Janet Gough/Celebrity Photo; page 4: Gail/A.P.R.F./Shooting Star; page 5: P. Adress/A.P.R.F./Shooting Star; page. 6: Bernhard Kuhmstedt/Retna; page 7: Steve Granitz/Retna; page 8: Rita Black/Shooting Star; page 9: Steve Granitz/Retna (top); Ron Gooman/Shooting Star (bottom); page 10: Ron Davis/Shooting Star (left); London Features (right); page 11: Paul Fenton/Shooting Star (top left); John Spellman/Retna (top right); Clavel/A.P.R.F./Shooting Star (bottom left); Max Smith/Retna (bottom right); page 12: Clavel/A.P.R.F./Shooting Star (top); John Spellman/Retna (bottom left); Bernhard Kuhmstedt/Retna (bottom right); page 13: Steve Granitz/Retna (bottom left); Kari Sellards/Shooting Star (bottom middle); Gary Gershoff/Retna (bottom right); page 14: Clavel/A.P.R.F./Shooting Star (top left); Mary Monaco/Shooting Star (top right); Bob Berg/Retna (bottom); page 15: Bernhard Kuhmstedt/Retna (top); Steve Granitz/Retna (middle); Paul Fenton/Shooting Star (bottom); page 16: Clavel/A.P.R.F./Shooting Star (top left); Bob Berg/Retna (bottom left); Kari Sellards/Shooting Star (top right); Jim Smeal/Ron Galella Ltd. (bottom right); page 17: Bernhard Kuhmstedt/Retna (top left); Bernhard Kuhmstedt/Retna (top right); Mary Monaco/Shooting Star (middle right); Kari Sellards/Shooting Star (bottom right); page 18: Clavel/A.P.R.F./Shooting Star; Page 19: Mitchell Layton/Retna (top left); Paul Fenton/Shooting Star (middle left); Kari Sellards/Shooting Star (bottom left); Mary Monaco/Shooting Star (top right); page 20: Melanie Edwards (top); Bernhard Kuhmstedt/Retna (bottom); page 21: Kari Sellards/Shooting Star (top); Paul Fenton/Shooting Star (bottom); page 22: Bob Berg/Retna (top); Neal Preston/Retna (bottom left); Bob Berg/Retna (bottom right); page 23: Paul Fenton/Shooting Star; page 25: Melanie Edwards/Retna (left); Max Smith/Retna (right); page 26: Michael Schreiber/Retna; page 27: Bernhard Kuhmstedt/Retna; page 28: Bernhard Kuhmstedt/Retna; page 28: Bernhard Kuhmstedt/Retna; page 29: John Spellman/Retna; page 30: Bob Berg/Retna; page 31: Bernhard Kuhmstedt/Retna; page 32: Steve Granitz/Retna; page 33: Jim Smeal/Ron Galella Ltd.; page 34: Caserta/A.P.R.F./Shooting Star; page 35: Kari Sellards/Shooting Star; page 36: Janet Gough/Celebrity Photo; page 37: Clavel/A.P.R.F./Shooting Star; page 38: Clavel/A.P.R.F./Shooting Star (left); page 39: Clavel/A.P.R.F/Shooting Star; page 40: Clavel/A.P.R.F./Shooting Star; page 41: Clavel/A.P.R.F./Shooting Star; page 42: Steve Granitz/Retna; page 43: Janet Gough/Celebrity Photo; page 44: Kari Sellards/Shooting Star; page 45: Paul Fenton/Shooting Star; page 46: Steve Granitz/Retna; page 47: London Features; page 48: Gail/A.P.R.F./Shooting Star.

ISBN 0-439-22220-6

Copyright © 2000 Scholastic Inc. All rights reserved.
Published by Scholastic Inc. SCHOLASTIC and associated logos are
trademarks and/or registered trademarks of Scholastic Inc.

Cover and interior design by Louise Bova

12 11 10 9 8 7 6 5 4 3 2 1   0 1 2 3 4 5 6/0
Printed in the U.S.A.
First Scholastic printing, August 2000

GUIDE TO WHAT'S INSIDE

Chapter One: Flashback: The Beginning 5

Chapter Two: Let's Hear It for the Boys! 10

Chapter Three: Lucky Lads 21

Chapter Four: All Aboard the S.S. 'N Sync 24

Chapter Five: No Strings Attached.......................31

Chapter Six: Extracurricular Activities 35

Chapter Seven: 'Nside 'N Sync...........................39

Chapter Eight: Predictions..............................43

Chapter Nine: Discography..............................45

Chapter Ten: How to Reach Them 47

JOEY

JC

JUSTIN

CHRIS

LANCE

WELCOME TO 'N SYNC — NOW AND FOREVER!

How much do fans love 'N Sync?

How 'bout — enough to catapult the band right into the history books!

How'd they do it? Only by snaring the band's second album, *No Strings Attached*, so fast, that it sold over ONE MILLION copies the FIRST DAY it came out.

And that has never been done before. Hence, history!

Clearly, Justin, JC, Lance, Chris, and Joey have the most loyal and dedicated fans on the planet.

Which brings us to this scrapbook. It's packed with cool pics and fabulous 'N Sync moments. And it's also filled with fascinating "inside 'N Sync" info!

Then there's the KEEPSAKE part. In most chapters, there's space and places for you to jot down your feelings and record your private moments with the boys.

And last but not least, there's that word FOREVER. The way things are going now, it looks like this fabulous fivesome could go on and on and on. Your memories of each and every moment you've had with Justin, Joey, Lance, Chris, and JC will live on, too — in the pages of this scrapbook.

Chapter One

FLASHBACK: THE BEGINNING

'N Sync's story is all about commitment, support, and dedication. But most of all, it's about the friendship of five very special and talented guys. Justin Randall Timberlake, Christopher Alan Kirkpatrick, Joseph Anthony Fatone Jr., James Lance Bass, and Joshua Scott Chasez aren't related, didn't grow up together, and weren't introduced to one another through a record producer or manager. In fact, their meeting was one quarter accident and about three quarters destiny.

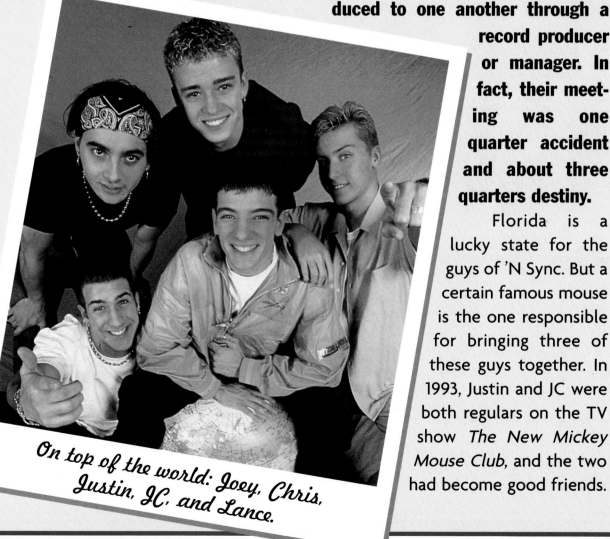

On top of the world: Joey, Chris, Justin, JC, and Lance.

Florida is a lucky state for the guys of 'N Sync. But a certain famous mouse is the one responsible for bringing three of these guys together. In 1993, Justin and JC were both regulars on the TV show *The New Mickey Mouse Club*, and the two had become good friends.

The show featured music and dance numbers, as well as comedy skits and short films. Once in a while, *MMC* needed extra performers to dance during the closing song. Joey auditioned, and became one of those lucky dancers. He met Justin and JC on the set, and the three soon became fast friends.

Fast forward a bit. Joey snagged a job working at Orlando's Universal Studios in a music and dance group called the Hollywood Hi-Tones. Chris had also won a role in the group. Joey introduced Chris to Justin and JC, and soon they'd all become the best of buds. The foursome could be spotted at local nightclubs, dancing up a storm. Their cool hip-hop moves inspired massive praise from their peers. Everyone wanted to know what group they were in and where they would be performing.

That gave Chris an idea. If the four friends were such a hot attraction on the dance floor, then forming a band that would incorporate their harmonizing voices seemed like the next logical step. There was just one

Laughing it up: These five guys aren't just bandmates, they're also good friends.

problem. They needed an additional voice to make the group complete. In short, they needed a "bass."

Turned out that Justin's old vocal coach knew the perfect match to turn this foursome into a fivesome. James Lance Bass had the look, the moves, and of course, the right sound. At the time, teenage Lance was singing in a competition choir called Attache in Mississippi. But after several phone calls with Justin and the guys, he convinced his folks to let him fly down to Orlando and check it out. That first meeting proved to be historic. It was more than the start of a new friendship — it was the birth of a band.

It takes the guys only two days to learn a dance routine.

The Name Game

So now they were a group — but one important element was still missing. These guys needed a name! Fortunately, Justin's mother came up with a great idea. She took the last initials from all the boys' first names: JustiN, ChriS, JoeY, LansteN (Lance's nickname), and JC. It was sheer coincidence that the word spelled 'N SYNC. But it made sense. That one word sums up the relationship between these five guys — they are always in perfect synch.

The next year went by in a blur. 'N Sync spent endless hours perfecting their voices, harmonizing, dancing, finding the right material, putting together a demo tape, and looking for representation. They even made a videotape of themselves performing at Disney World's Pleasure Island. And their hard work quickly paid off.

By 1996, they had secured a manager, signed a record deal with RCA, and released their first single ("I Want You Back") in Europe. In 1998,

Justin's mom told them, "When you sing together, you're really in synch." The guys played with the idea and realized the letters of their names formed 'N Sync.

they were ready to take on their home shores. 'N Sync opened for Janet Jackson on her Velvet Rope tour, and they released their self-titled album, *'N Sync*, which became a number one smash. The rest is, well, history.

FLASHBACK: YOUR BACK STORY
Fill in your own special 'N Sync memories.

How I first heard about 'N Sync: _____

How old I was: _____

I first saw 'N Sync (on TV, in concert): _____

The first 'N Sync song I heard was: _____

My reaction to it was: _____

I thought the guys looked: _____

What I liked best about the group was: _____

Right away I thought the cutest boy was: _____

I liked him best because: _____

If I could date one of the boys, it would be: _____

My ideal date would consist of: _____

Clip Your Favorite 'N Sync Photo Here:

'N Sync shows off their killer dance moves.

9

Chapter Two

LET'S HEAR IT FOR THE BOYS!

JUSTIN:

At nineteen years old, Justin is still nicknamed "the baby" by his fellow bandmates. Born on January 31, 1981, in Memphis, Tennessee, Justin was only seven years old when he and his mom, Lynn, moved to Orlando, Florida. He showed a passion for music and performing early on — "If I could talk, I could sing. I was always performing for somebody," he says. In his first year in Orlando, he entered tons of dancing and singing contests. At one called "Dance Like the New Kids on the Block" — in honor of 1989's mega-popular fivesome — Justin nabbed first place.

But Justin didn't rely solely on his natural talent. He also studied the piano and guitar, took voice lessons, and participated in as many local and school shows as he could fit into his busy schedule. His big break came at the early age of twelve, when he was recruited by the folks at Disney to join their show, *The New Mickey Mouse Club*.

True or false? Justin's involved with singer and former MMC castmate Britney Spears. Justin won't say!

Justin likes to have his microphone very close to his mouth when he's singing.

TASTY TIDBIT: Justin's favorite ice cream is chocolate mocha chip.

JUST JUSTIN

Name: Justin Randall Timberlake
Birthday: January 31, 1981
Zodiac Sign: Aquarius
Birthplace: Memphis, Tennessee
Hair color: Blond
Eye color: Blue
Height : 5'11"
Parents: Lynn and Randall, stepdad
Siblings: Half brothers, Jonathan and Steven
Pets: A dog named Ozzie; a cat named Alley

Justin could sing before he could talk — he has perfect pitch.

TOP 4 FEARS	**YOUR TOP 4 FEARS**
1. Sharks	1. _____
2. Spiders	2. _____
3. Snakes	3. _____
4. Going into the ocean	4. _____

Justin used to sing in church. Later on, he did country music!

Justin's advice for kids interested in becoming musicians? "Practice, practice, practice."

11

COOL QUOTE: Chris's idea of a perfect date? "Anything just spontaneous."

CHRIS:

At twenty-eight, Chris often plays the role of "big bro" in the group. But though he may be wise and mature in some ways, he also loves silly gags and jokes — in fact, his bandmates nicknamed him "the prankster." Chris was born on October 17, 1971, in Clarion, Pennsylvania. As a child, he dreamed of becoming the next Gene Kelly (a famous actor/dancer/singer from the '40s and '50s). He performed in every high school play or musical he could make time for. After graduation, Chris attended Rollins College. He planned to study psychology, but his love of music brought him to a crossroads. Chris courageously decided to follow his heart, and auditioned for an acting gig at Universal Studios. At twenty-one, he snagged a part in a group called the Hollywood Hi-Tones, where he sang old '50s-style doo-wop songs. It was this job that introduced him to Joey, and eventually gave him the idea to form 'N Sync.

DID YOU KNOW: Chris was cast in the lead role of his high school musical *Oliver!*

Chris was born to skate!

CRAZY ABOUT CHRIS

Name: Christopher Alan Kirkpatrick
Birthday: October 17, 1971
Zodiac Sign: Libra
Birthplace: Clarion, Pennsylvania
Hair color: Brown
Eye color: Brown
Height: 5'8"
Parents: Mom, Beverly
Siblings: Half sisters, Molly, Kate, Emily, and Taylor

Chris is crazy about his dog, Busta.

GETTING PERSONAL

Worst memory:
The death of his father
Prized possession:
His Rollerblades and surfboard
Best childhood friend:
Angelo

YOUR TURN

Worst memory:
_____

Prized possession:
_____

Best childhood friend:
_____

"I believe in the idea of love at first sight. I don't think you can fall in love with someone if you don't know them, but I believe you can have a connection that can turn into love."

JOEY:

Born in Brooklyn, New York, on January 28, 1977, Joey fell in love with performing early on, and was putting on shows for his family and friends at age 3. He inherited his love of singing from his dad, who sang in a group called the Orlons in the '50s. Joey still considers his dad his biggest musical influence.

Joey's big break came at age 13, when his family moved to Orlando. A few years later, while still in high school, he landed the gig at Universal Studios. It was the best day of his life! Before he made it big

with 'N Sync, Joey had small roles on the TV show *SeaQuest DSV*, and in the movies *Once Upon a Time in America* and *Matinee*. He still loves acting, and is working on a handbook for young actors with his former drama teacher.

FACT NOT FICTION: If Joey could relive one day in his own life, he says it would be the day he graduated from high school. "It was happy and sad at the same time . . . very emotional."

Joey is the band's resident flirt.

Joey loves to dance up a storm and go clubbing!

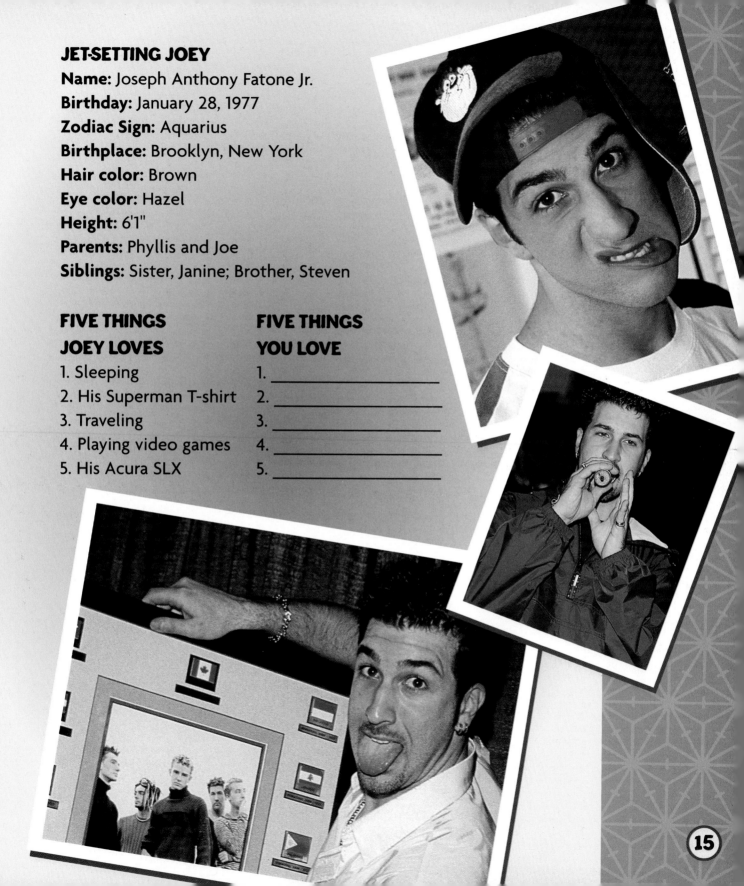

JET-SETTING JOEY

Name: Joseph Anthony Fatone Jr.
Birthday: January 28, 1977
Zodiac Sign: Aquarius
Birthplace: Brooklyn, New York
Hair color: Brown
Eye color: Hazel
Height: 6'1"
Parents: Phyllis and Joe
Siblings: Sister, Janine; Brother, Steven

FIVE THINGS JOEY LOVES

1. Sleeping
2. His Superman T-shirt
3. Traveling
4. Playing video games
5. His Acura SLX

FIVE THINGS YOU LOVE

1. _____
2. _____
3. _____
4. _____
5. _____

*JC says — "I'm a boring guy —
I just like sttting in the studio."
Boring? Nuh-uh!*

JC:

Originally from the Washington, DC, area, JC was born on August 8, 1976. His family moved to Maryland when he was tiny. At school he excelled in sports, especially football and baseball. But he soon found his real passion was for singing and dancing. When JC was 15, a friend suggested he audition for *The New Mickey Mouse Club*. He did, and won the role that changed his life forever. *MMC* really prepared JC for his future in music. He learned how to work in a fast-paced environment, to enjoy rehearsing, and to be very, very disciplined.

At twenty-three, JC is the most laid back member of 'N Sync. He's also been the brunt of more than a few practical jokes from his bandmates. Once they took pictures of him with Rollo candies coming out of his ears while JC was sleeping on a plane! JC loves napping so much, his comrades sometimes call him "Mr. Sleepy." However, JC is totally the opposite onstage: He's energized, hyped-up, and ready to rock!

DID YOU KNOW: JC's most prized possession is his Hard Rock Cafe menu collection.

JOYFULLY JC

Name: Joshua Scott Chasez
Birthday: August 8, 1976
Zodiac Sign: Leo
Birthplace: Washington, DC
Hair color: Brown
Eye color: Blue-hazel
Height: 6'1"
Parents: Karen and Roy
Siblings: Brother, Tyler, Sister, Heather

JC says: "I believe there's someone out there for everyone."

JC is happiest producing: "I love creating the stuff people are going to hear over and over."

JC'S FAVORITE FOODS

1. Veggie: Broccoli
2. Dinner: Chinese
3. Cereal: Life
4. Jelly bean flavors: Cotton Candy, Root Beer, Pear
5. Cookie: Double-stuffed Oreos

YOUR FAVORITE FOODS

1. _____
2. _____
3. _____
4. _____
5. _____

LANCE:

James Lance Bass was born in Laurel, Mississippi, on May 4, 1979, and lived there until he was 11, when his family moved to the neighboring town of Clinton. Lance was a real "doer" in high school — he was an active member of the student council and the honor society, and he was even elected president of his class. But the one club that changed Lance's life was chorus. It introduced him to his true love: music.

Lance toured for a while with a musical group called Attache. He contemplated becoming an astronaut, and even passed NASA's entrance examination. But then he got "the call" — his vocal teacher suggested he meet with a gang of guys in Orlando, Florida, who seemed rather serious about starting a band. Lance went to Florida to meet Justin, JC, Joey, and Chris. All it took was one meeting, and, well, you know the rest! It's history.

COOL QUOTE: "If I have a girlfriend, I want to be there for her — and be the best boyfriend I can be."

FACT NOT FICTION: Lance once worked as a vocal coach.

LUCKY LANCE

Name: James Lance Bass

Birthday: May 4, 1979

Zodiac Sign: Taurus

Birthplace: Laurel, Mississippi

Hair color: Blond

Eye color: Blue — but sometimes they look hazel

Height: 5'10"

Parents: Diane and Jim

Siblings: Sister, Stacy

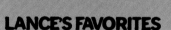

Lance is the group's resident beach bum.

LANCE'S FAVORITES

Color: Candy Apple Red

TV show: *Friends*

Cartoon Character: the Tazmanian Devil

Actress: Jennifer Aniston

Actor: Tom Hanks

Food: French toast

Drink: Dr Pepper

YOUR FAVORITES

1. _____
2. _____
3. _____
4. _____
5. _____
6. _____
7. _____

YOUR TURN:

Name: _____

Birthday: _____

Zodiac Sign: _____

Birthplace: _____

Hair color: _____

Eye color: _____

Height : _____

Parents: _____

Siblings: _____

Pets: _____

Joey with his family — brother Steven, sister Janine, mom Phyllis, and dad Joe.

Chapter Three

LUCKY LADS

Do you have a good luck charm or a person you feel lucky to have in your life? The members of 'N Sync are no different — they do too!

JC wears his good luck charm on a black rope around his neck. He's worn it for the past six years and never takes it off. The only time he did was when the band rehearsed their first video, "I Want You Back." But he felt so uneasy without it, he *had* to put it back on during the taping.

JUSTIN says the *people* in his life are his lucky charms. That includes his family and of course, his music pals. But this luck thing works both ways — his bandmates and family feel lucky to have *him* in their lives, too!

LANCE has a special silver bracelet. He's worn it for the past two years. It was given to him by rappers in the Sugar Hill Gang, and has a lot of personal meaning. He never takes it off.

JOEY carries a miniature four-leaf clover statuette around with him everywhere. It has a little face and the word "lucky" printed on it. It was a gift from his best friend from school, Eric. Joey's famous Superman charm never leaves his neck.

CHRIS claims he doesn't have a lucky charm, but that doesn't stop him from wearing lots of necklaces. They're his prized possessions! In fact, he feels weird without them. Chris is definitely the least superstitious of the group, but he does admit to believing in angels. "I think everyone has somebody watching over them," he says.

SILLY SUPERSTITIONS:
• Justin doesn't like to walk under ladders.
• JC's careful around mirrors. Break one, and it's seven years of bad luck. Ouch!
• At 3:33, P.M. or A.M., Lance likes to make a wish and kiss the ceiling.

Before each concert, the boys have a quick round of Hackey Sack. It's become their lucky, pre-show ritual.

Joey always wears his Superman necklace.

YOUR TURN: LUCKY FOR YOU

I can't live without: _____

_____

_____

It was given to me by: _____

_____

The number of years I've had it: _____

_____

It's important to me because: _____

_____

_____

_____

_____

_____

_____

_____

_____

Chapter Four

ALL ABOARD THE S.S. 'N SYNC

The year 1999 started out with a bang for the boys of 'N Sync. They went on a seven-month concert tour called "Ain't No Stopping Us Now." The concerts

sold out in a matter of minutes, and the guys couldn't have been more thrilled. In fact, they were as excited about the tour as their fans were. They actually sailed onstage in a huge boat, dressed as sailors, singing Christopher Cross's famous song, "Sailing."

The tour kicked off on January 1, 1999, in Las Vegas, and went nonstop until May 15, when the guys "docked" in Fort Lauderdale, Florida. They "sailed" through more then twenty-five states — singing, dancing, and bringing down the house. 'N Sync even "sailed" the high seas, visiting Hawaii and Great Britain. The guys took a short breather in June to regroup and catch up on some much needed zzzzz's. Then it was onto another two months of summer touring.

The band loves performing, and however tired they might be, they never mind long bus rides, the grueling schedule, or the endless hours of rehearsals.

It was a real treat to sing in front of their adoring fans. As Joey says, "The best thing [is], we get to meet a lot of our fans and perform in front of thousands and thousands and thousands of people."

YOUR TURN: WHEN I SAW 'N SYNC IN CONCERT

I saw 'N Sync in concert
[where & when]:_____

I was with [friends, family]: _____

My favorite song they
sang was: _____

They were wearing: _____

The first song they
performed was: _____

My favorite part was:_____

The concert will always be
special to me because: _____
_____

Lance says: "If we didn't have the fans we have, it would be so boring for us. There's so much energy at our concerts that you can just feed off it."

BOYS ON TV — AND IN THE MOVIES

When the guys aren't performing in front of a live audience, they are busy acting in front of cameras. They have made guest-star appearances on TV favorites *Clueless* and *Sabrina the Teenage Witch*. The gang also got a shot at the silver screen, winning cameos in the movie *Jack of All Trades*. Joey and JC were cast as pizza makers, Chris played a bad guy who steals pizza from the shop owner, and Lance played a flight engineer. While *Jack of All Trades* was filming, Justin was busy preparing for his role in a made-for-TV-movie called *Model Behavior*, which aired March 2000, while Lance played Beverley Mitchell's love interest on an episode of *7th Heaven*. The guys are also planning a movie they'll all be doing together. Says Joey, "It basically takes place in high school, and we'll all be playing parts — not ourselves."

JC says: "Our fans [are] awesome, I think they must be the most energetic people on the face of the earth. And we love that. So our fans inspire us."

The gang sang holiday tunes like "Love's in Our Hearts on Christmas Day" with Rosie O'Donnell, and even helped light the gigantic Christmas tree at Rockefeller Center in New York City. They performed their hit single "Bye, Bye, Bye" on *Saturday Night Live* — and even spoofed themselves in one of the skits. Naturally, they're total *TRL* regulars.

CHARITABLE CHUMS

Possibly the only thing larger than 'N Sync's talent is their hearts. They love to lend a helping hand — or voice — to good causes.

'N Sync have visited with teens to discuss the Columbine High School shooting in Littleton, CO, and also went to the hospital to talk with the victims. They've hosted a charity basketball game; performed at the World AIDS Day convention; worked with the Make a Wish Foundation; sang at Nickelodeon's Help-A-Thon; and in October 1999, graced the lawn of the White House for a televised concert to benefit the Save the Music Foundation. And probably the group's wackiest gift to charity came when NY radio station WHTZ auctioned off Justin's half-eaten slice of French toast on eBay for $1,025! The proceeds went to charity, along with a matching gift from the station.

FACT NOT FICTION: Justin set up The Justin Timberlake Foundation, a program that raises money for music and arts education in schools. Last winter, he met the President and First Lady while visiting Washington to promote his foundation. Hillary Clinton got into the act, giving her seal of approval and pledging total support for the program.

CUTTING LOOSE

Most of 1999 was smooth sailing. But in September, the band announced that they were leaving their record company, RCA, and the company that had arranged their deal with RCA, Trans-Continental Records.. "We felt like they [the people at TransCon] were taking rather than giving," Justin told *USA Today*. "So we rearranged the situation."

The band wanted to go to Jive Records, the company that makes Britney Spears' and the Backstreet Boys' records. But the move was not an easy one. And RCA and TransCon slapped 'N Sync with a big lawsuit. That meant they'd have to put their careers and music on hold. They wouldn't be able to release their long-awaited next album. There was also talk that the band would have to give up their name. For a moment, 'N Sync thought their lives would never be the same.

TAKING ACTION

'N Sync has an army of dedicated fans, and they did everything possible to help out. Through the Internet, fans organized rallies protesting the lawsuit in New York City and Orlando, Florida. Fans also signed petitions asking Congress to help protect young performers and artists from being taken advantage of by managers and record companies.

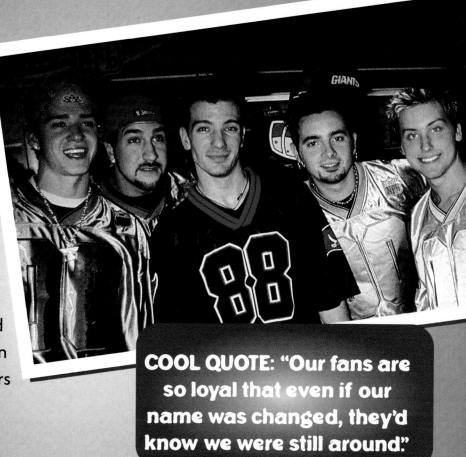

COOL QUOTE: "Our fans are so loyal that even if our name was changed, they'd know we were still around."

YOUR TURN:

If the band had to change
their name, I'd suggest: _____

If I was going to protest

something, it would be: _____

I feel most strongly about: _____

BONDING

Because of the lawsuit, 'N Sync went through several months of uncertainty and difficulty. But the bad vibes did not affect the friendship between the five band members at all. In fact, it was just the opposite. It's no secret that the guys have always been tight. And the split with RCA only brought them closer together. They were more determined than ever to go forward with their new album, even if it meant they'd have to do it on their own. And they did.

Chapter Five

NO STRINGS ATTACHED

Because they had no record company or representation, the boys decided to scrap an album they'd been working on for RCA and make an album, *No Strings Attached*, on their own. "We wanted to do it our way from top to bottom," JC says. The guys were responsible for creating every single aspect of it. They conceived the idea for the record, came up with the theme, searched for the songs to record, and when they couldn't find ones they liked, wrote

The guys try their hand as producers in the recording studio.

their own. They hired producers for all the songs and even designed the artwork on the cover. Basically, they became the album's executive producers.

No Strings Attached took two years to make. As you can guess, the guys are proudest of this album, since they threw their entire hearts and souls into making it. And it definitely paid off. The album sold a record one million copies on its first day, and 2.42 million copies in its first week. (These killers sales made *No Strings Attached* the best-selling album release of ALL TIME.) Way to go, guys!

FACT NOT FICTION:

- JC wrote the songs "No Strings Attached," "Digital Getdown," and "Space Cowboy."
- The tune "Good for You" was penned by Justin!
- 'N Sync performs the ballad "I Thought She Knew" a cappella.

SONGS FROM THE HEART

"Bye, Bye, Bye" was released on January 17, 2000. And from the second it hit the airwaves, the song was a total smash. The guys say the song is a "dude's" version of "Girl Power."

There's a lot of meaning behind those lyrics. "Bye, Bye, Bye" is not just about saying *ciao* to an old girlfriend, it's about leaving behind everyone who tried to hold the guys back from reaching their goals.

'N SYNC's Favorite Songs:

Justin: "God Must Have Spent a Little More Time on You"
Lance: "God Must Have Spent a Little More Time on You"
JC: "Noel" and "Holy Night," from 'N Sync's album *Home for Christmas*
Chris: "Sailing"
Joey: "I Drive Myself Crazy"

My favorite:

Backstage at the Forum in L.A.:
It's all a piece of cake.

Justin, JC, Lance, Chris, and Joey proudly display these plaques, awarded for selling their millionth record.

A NEW BEGINNING

'N Sync won preliminary hearings in their lawsuit, and eventually ended up settling out of court. But there is no question that the guys ended up as winners. They'd get to keep their name, release their album, and even switch record companies. Jive signed them on immediately, no questions asked. Everyone was thrilled.

Even though Jive handles the Backstreet Boys, there's no competition between the two bands — at least, not as far as 'N Sync is concerned. Justin had this to say about 'N Sync's breaking the Backstreet Boys' *Millennium* sales record:

The boys would love to star in their own movie. A Saturday Night Live meets Wayne's World, or Swingers meets The Outsiders.

"I don't think we ever felt like we were in their shadow. We have our own thing going on. It's just that with this album title, we took such a bold approach that people started to recognize it." What 'N Sync love most about their new label is that the company is totally open to their ideas. Jive works closely with the band and asks for their creative input on everything.

VIDEO-RAMA: In the video for "Bye, Bye, Bye," the fivesome are puppets who have been cut loose from their strings. They're being chased by an evil supermodel who's trying to get the guys back and make them into puppets again.

Chapter Six

EXTRACURRICULAR ACTIVITIES

Even through the band is tighter than ever, that doesn't mean they don't work independently on various projects. This year the guys really put the pedal to the metal, and sent their creative energy in lots of different directions. Because they're so close, there's never any jealousy or competition. Just lots of support and encouragement. Here's just a sample of what the individual band members are up to:

JC: In addition to writing three very cool songs for the *No Strings Attached* album, JC is currently writing, producing, and collaborating with other artists and bands, including Britney Spears, Blagu, and Wild Orchid. He's already written three songs for Wild Orchid's album, one of which is called "Fire."

CHRIS: The most entrepreneurial of the group, and a huge fan of fashion, Chris founded and became the CEO of his own clothing line for guys and girls. It's called FuMan Skeeto Enterprises. Of course, his bandmates will be modeling his new duds every chance they get! FuMan is also the name of Chris' new production company, which he

No matter what other projects they take on, music will __always__ come first.

'N Sync got dressed up for the Grammys 2000 — they were nominated for "Best Pop Collaboration" for the song "Music of My Heart," with Gloria Estefan.

hopes will help new recording artists jumpstart their careers.

LANCE: You'd think that managing two up-and-coming country singers, Meredith Edwards and Jack Defoe, as part of his FreeLance Enterprises management company would keep Lance more than busy, right? Not a chance. Last year, Lance tried his hand at acting, and got to go on an onscreen date with *7th Heaven* star Beverley Mitchell. Lance got together with his buddy Beverley for dinner one night, and she just happened to mention that she wanted to have a boyfriend on the show. Lance volunteered for the part. His performance was so awesome that the network promised he'd appear again in the show's finale. He's also busy working on a screenplay with Joey, who's caught the acting bug.

JOEY: This year, Joey had his nose in a book — an acting book, that is. He's financing and overseeing the creation of an acting handbook for students across the country, written by his former drama coach. Joey also traveled back to Orlando to teach an improvisation class called "Spotlight on U" for teens interested in acting.

JUSTIN: The youngest 'N Syncer took center stage this year, but this time it was in front of a movie camera. He won a leading role as a cute male model in Disney's TV movie *Model Behavior*. The movie is about two teen girls — both played by *Party of Five*'s Maggie Lawson — who trade places. One is a super-model, the other, a self-described nerd. Justin's character is supposed to be dating the model, but soon finds himself falling for the average teen.

YOUR TURN:

These are the projects I'm
planning for the future:_____

_____

The most exciting thing
that's happened to me this year was:_____

My goals for this year are: _____

_____

_____

_____

Justin would be interested in doing professional modeling.

Chris's new look rocks!

NEW YEAR, NEW LOOKS, AND NEW LOCKS

Justin colored his signature curls from blond to brown.

Chris said bye, bye, bye to his long locks.

Joey added fire-engine red streaks to his hair. The new look was hot!

Lance colored his hair brown and added blond highlights.

JC got a new hip style. He slicked his hair back and added a little color, too.

VOTE: Whose new look do you like most and why?

_____

_____

_____

_____

_____

_____

_____

_____

Chapter Seven

'NSIDE 'N SYNC

Sure you know tons of info on the guys, but here's some hot stats that may be new to you. For instance . . .

LANCE
- Had braces.
- Has an innie belly button.
- Loves water-skiing.
- Loves pajamas more than any other type of clothing.
- Earned the nickname "Scoop" because he always knows the band's schedule.

YOUR TURN:
My nickname is:_____
The person who gave
 it to me was: _____
I earned it because I:

_____

Lance says, "I would love to die in a horror movie."

CHRIS
- Prefers sunsets to sunrises.
- Sings songs by Busta Rhymes and Brian McKnight in the shower.

Joey on clubbing: *"I go out after a show to let off some steam. I love going out to clubs."*

• Wishes he were a little taller.

• Fears heights.

• Has a scar over his left eye, which he got by accidentally running into a wall while chasing his sister when they were little.

YOUR TURN:

In the shower I sing: _____

I have a scar: _____

I got it when I: _____

JUSTIN

• Got his first kiss in the 6th grade — he was very nervous about it.

• Has never snowboarded.

• Bought his mom a white gold bracelet with a diamond for Christmas.

• Learned to dance from watching MTV.

• Is inspired by Michael Jordan because of what he's achieved and because he's never given up.

• Would fill a time capsule with a microphone, a guitar, the band's American Music Award, a pair of sneakers, and a tabloid paper — just to prove that he got through all the hard stuff in 1999.

YOUR TURN:

Five objects I'd put in a time capsule:

1. _____
2. _____
3. _____
4. _____
5. _____

JC's favorite songs? "Fragile" and "Shape of My Heart," by Sting, and "Violet," by Seal.

JOEY

- Loves poetry.
- Used to play Wolfman in the Beetlejuice show at Universal Studios, Florida.
- Would like to spend a day as Robert DeNiro — just to see what makes the great actor tick.

YOUR TURN

If I could spend the day as a different person, I'd choose: _____
Because: _____

JC

- Has attended not one, not two, but FIVE proms.
- Used to carry his five pet chameleons with him to school in his pocket.
- Considers his family and friends his most prized possessions.
- Would be "Sleepy Spice" if he were a Spice Girl.
- Considers Seal, Sting, and Boyz II Men his musical inspirations.

YOUR TURN

I'm inspired by: _____

Because: _____

_____

Chapter Eight

PREDICTIONS

It's been a wild and wacky, but never boring ride since 'N Sync exploded onto the music scene in 1998. The difficult times have made everything they have now that much sweeter. They're more than happy with their new record company. Their album is sleek, cool, and is already breaking records as one of the biggest-selling and most popular albums of all time. Who could ask for anything more? These days, the future's looking brighter than the sun.

For sure: *No Strings Attached* is 'N Sync's most respected and popular album to date. Plus, they have new songs on two movie soundtracks —"Somewhere, Someday" appears on the soundtrack of *Pokemon the Second Movie: The Power of One,* and "Through Heaven's Eyes" is on the *Light It Up* soundtrack.

'N Sync at the 1999 Blockbuster Awards.

NOMINATIONS & AWARDS:

The band was nominated for a slew of awards this year, including:

•Nickelodeon's 13th Annual Kid's Choice Awards, "Favorite musical Group" and "Favorite Song From a Movie" for "Music of My Heart"

•The Grammys, Best Pop Collaboration With Vocals for "Music of My Heart" (with Gloria Estefan) and Best Country Collaboration With Vocals for "God Must Have Spent a Little More Time on You" (with Alabama)

•Academy Award, "Music of My Heart," (with Gloria Estefan) from the movie *Music of the Heart,* for best original song

•Blockbuster Entertainment Awards, "Favorite Group", "Best Song From a Movie" for "Music of My Heart"

VOTE: YOUR 'N SYNC NOMINATIONS:

Coolest Hairdo: _____

Best Looking: _____

Best Dressed: _____

Best Vocalist: _____

Best Dancer: _____

At home for Christmas: The band that bakes together, stays together!

Chapter Nine

DISCOGRAPHY

NO STRINGS ATTACHED: **released March 21, 2000**

1. "Bye, Bye, Bye"
2. "It's Gonna Be Me"
3. "Space Cowboy"
4. "Just Got Paid"
5. "Makes Me Ill"
6. "This I Promise You"
7. "No Strings Attached"
8. "Digital Getdown"
9. "Bringin' Da Noise"
10. "That's When I'll Stop Loving You"
11. "Good for You"
12. "I Thought She Knew"

IC says that in the studio, "Ideas don't get shot down, they get improved on — that's what the group is all about."

'N SYNC: **released in March 1998**

1. "Tearin' Up My Heart"
2. "I Just Wanna Be With You"
3. "Here We Go"
4. "For the Girl Who Has Everything"
5. "God Must Have Spent a Little More Time on You"
6. "You Got It"
7. "I Need Love"

8. "I Want You Back"

9. "Everything I Own"

10. "I Drive Myself Crazy"

11. "Craze for You"

12. "Sailing"

13. "Giddy Up"

HOME FOR CHRISTMAS: **released in November 1998**

1. "The First Noel"

2. "The Christmas Song"

3. "This Christmas"

4. "Holy Night"

5. "I Never Knew the Meaning of Christmas"

6. "Love's in Our Hearts on Christmas Day"

7. "Under My Tree"
8. "I Hear Angels"
9. "Will You Be Mine This Christmas"
10. "It's Christmas"
11. "In Love on Christmas"
12. "Home for Christmas"

Lance says Gloria Estefan, who the band collaborated with on "Music of My Heart," could be the sixth member of 'N Sync.

MUSICAL COLLABORATIONS:

1. "Music of the Heart" — with Gloria Estefan
2. "God Must Have Spent a Little More Time on You" — with Alabama
3. "Space Cowboy" — with TLC's Lisa "Left Eye" Lopes
4. "Bring It All to Me" — with Blaque
5. "Sailing" — with Christopher Cross
6. "Trashin' the Camp" — Phil Collins (from the *Tarzan* soundtrack)

YOUR TURN:
Three people or groups I'd love to see perform with 'N Sync:

1. _____
2. _____
3. _____

Chapter Ten

HOW TO REACH THEM

Heads up! 'N Sync has some new numbers, addresses, and web sites.

Snail Mail:

'N Sync
Jive Records
137-139 West 25th Street
New York, NY 10001

'N Sync Fan Club
PO Box 5248
Bellingham, WA 98227

Web Sites:

•   The new official web page:
http://www.byebyebye.com;
http://www.nsync.com

•   Chris's clothing line:
http://FuManSkeeto.com

•   http://www.peeps.com/nsync2

What do the boys like best about being in 'N Sync? Joey said it best: "Being on tour, performing in front of thousands of people, and touching so many lives out there is the greatest feeling. Thanks for supporting us throughout the year and hopefully in years to come."

READ THE 'N SYNC COLLECTION!

'N Sync books by Scholastic!

Backstage Pass: 'N Sync

Backstage Pass: Just Justin

PopPeople: Justin Timberlake